discover
politics

Peter Joyce

*To my wife, Julie, and my daughters,
Emmeline and Eleanor*

Hodder Education

Hodder Education is an Hachette UK company

First published in UK 2011 by Hodder Education.

Copyright © 2011 Peter Joyce

The moral rights of the author have been asserted.
Database right Hodder Education (makers).

British Library Cataloguing in Publication Data: a catalogue record for this title
is available from the British Library.

10 9 8 7 6 5 4 3 2 1

The publisher has used its best endeavours to ensure that any website
addresses referred to in this book are correct and active at the time of going
to press. However, the publisher and the author have no responsibility for the
websites and can make no guarantee that a site will remain live or that the
content will remain relevant, decent or appropriate.

The publisher has made every effort to mark as such all words which it
believes to be trademarks. The publisher should also like to make it clear that
the presence of a word in the book, whether marked or unmarked, in no way
affects its legal status as a trademark.

Every reasonable effort has been made by the publisher to trace the copyright
holders of material in this book. Any errors or omissions should be notified in
writing to the publisher, who will endeavour to rectify the situation for any
reprints and future editions.

Hachette UK's policy is to use papers that are natural, renewable and
recyclable products and made from wood grown in sustainable forests.
The logging and manufacturing processes are expected to conform to the
environmental regulations of the country of origin.

www.hoddereducation.co.uk

Typeset by MPS Limited, a Macmillan Company.
Printed in Great Britain

Contents

1

key issues in the study of politics

We are all familiar with the term 'politics'. We associate it with taking decisions that relate to the way in which our country or neighbourhood should be run. It is encountered in the workplace, perhaps in the form of 'office politics'. It is also found in the home, perhaps involving the taking of financial decisions relating to the family budget. But what exactly is involved in the study of politics?

Our starting point for the study of politics is thus to understand what the subject is about. Therefore, this opening chapter defines the broad concerns of politics – what its main themes consist of – and goes on from that to consider some of the key terms with which we need to be familiar in order to embark upon our study of politics.

Having understood these terms, we are then in a position to move on and consider some of the more detailed aspects of political conduct.

Definition

Human relationships are crucial to the study of politics. Human beings do not live in isolation. We live in communities. These may be small (such as a family) or large (such as a country). Politics embraces the study of the behaviour of individuals within a group context. The focus of its study is broad and includes issues such as inter-group relationships, the management of groups, the operations of their collective decision-making processes (especially the activities and operations of the state) and the implementation and enforcement of decisions. The regulation of conflict between individuals and groups is a particular focus of political analysis, to which the study of the concept of power and the manner in which it is exercised is central. The study of politics thus involves a wide range of complementary subject areas which include political theory, political history, government and public administration, policy analysis and international relations.

In the following sections we discuss a number of key issues that relate to the study of politics. These are usually referred to as 'concepts' and they provide us with an underpinning on which a more detailed examination of the political process in liberal democracies can be built.

Political culture

We expect to see a number of common features in a liberal democratic political system. These include institutions such as a chief executive, legislatures and courts, organizations such as political parties and pressure groups, processes such as elections and the possession by individual citizens of a range of personal freedoms. However, their composition, conduct, powers, relationships and operations differ from one country to another. Within a common framework, the workings of the political system in each liberal democracy are subject to wide variation. In France, for example, there is a wide degree of tolerance for conflict as a means of settling political disputes. In Sweden, however, the spirit of compromise tends to guide the actions of key participants to the political process. In the United Kingdom there is a tradition of evolutionary rather than revolutionary change.

These differing attitudes influence the conduct of political activity by both politicians and the general public. When we refer to a country's political culture we are emphasizing the similarity of views held within any particular country. We are suggesting that within any one country there is a tendency for the majority of people to think, feel and act in a similar manner concerning the conduct of political affairs. But these sentiments may be quite different from the core values espoused by citizens in other liberal democracies.

States and governments

States and governments

A state consists of a wide range of permanent official institutions (such as the bureaucracy, police, courts, military, parliament and local government) which are responsible for the organization of communal life within specific geographic boundaries. These are usually referred to as a 'country' or 'nation' and the state enjoys sovereignty within them. Decisions that are taken in the name of the state are binding on all members of that society and may, if necessary, be enforced by the legitimate use of power to prevent, restrain or punish breaches of the law.

There are a wide range of views concerning the operations of the state. Liberal analysis suggests that the state is neutral and independent of any class interests. It arises out of the voluntary agreement of its members and serves impartially to mediate the conflicts which arise within society, seeking to promote the national interest above sectional concerns. Elite theorists, however, suggest political power is wielded by a ruling elite whose interests are maintained and advanced by the state. Marxism identifies this ruling elite as the economically powerful, the bourgeoisie, and views the state as a mechanism that will mediate between the conflict between capital and labour (which they assert to be inevitable) in order to sustain class exploitation and profit accumulation.

The term 'state' is often used synonomously with the term 'government'. This latter term refers to the institutions concerned with making, implementing and enforcing political decisions. In a narrower sense, however, government is often associated with those who wield executive power within a state, who give direction to its activities. In liberal democracies, political parties compete for control of the state and in this sense governments have a limited and temporary existence whereas states are permanent.

Power, authority and legitimacy

A major concern of a government is to secure the obedience of its citizens to its decisions. There are two broad explanations concerning why a government is able to secure popular compliance to its objectives or policies. These centre on an understanding of the concepts of power and authority.

Power

Power entails the ability to compel obedience. A body exercising power has the ability to invoke sanctions in order to secure compliance to its decisions. The fear of the sanction thus ensures that the body which may invoke it is able to achieve its goals. A government which possesses power is thus obeyed as its citizens are afraid of the consequences of disobedience. Dictatorships may often govern in such a fashion, executing those who dare disagree with their policies. In liberal democratic political structures, coercion is often coupled to resources at the government's disposal, enabling it to offer rewards as well as threats to secure obedience.

Authority

The second explanation to account for governments being able to exert control over their citizens is the authority possessed by such institutions. Authority is based on moral force. An individual or institution which possesses authority secures compliance to its suggestions primarily if there is general agreement that those who put forward such ideas have the right to propose and implement them. Citizens thus obey governments because there is a general consensus that it has the right to take decisions even if the content of them is not generally popular.

In liberal democratic political systems the political office occupied by those who give orders forms the main basis of their authority. We accept that presidents or prime ministers have the right to give orders by virtue of the public positions which they occupy. However, political leaders frequently derive their authority from more than one source: in Britain the association of the prime minister with government carried out in the name of the monarch gives this office holder authority derived from both traditional and legal-bureaucratic sources.

In liberal democracies governments possess both power and authority. They are obeyed partly because there is general consent that they have the right to govern, but also because the police, courts and penal system may be used as a sanction to force compliance to their laws. Power that is divorced from authority is likely to produce an unstable political structure in which violence, disorder and revolution threaten the existence of the government.

Legitimacy

Legitimacy entails popular acceptance of the exercise of power within a political system. Legitimacy is a quality that confers acceptance of the actions undertaken by the government from those who are subject to them. Those who are subject to such rules may not necessarily approve of them, but legitimacy involves an acceptance that the government has the right to make decisions and that the public has a duty to obey them.

In liberal democratic political systems, legitimacy is founded on the notion of popular consent. Governments derive their position from elections. This is a process in which all citizens are entitled to participate – and are required to if voting is compulsory. The support obtained at an election is the basis of a government's claim on the obedience of its citizens to the actions which it subsequently undertakes, provided that it acts in accordance within the established rules of political conduct. Legitimacy is important in establishing stable government able to draw upon the obedience of its citizens.

The rule of law

The rule of law suggests that citizens can only be punished by the state using formalized procedures when they have broken the law and that all citizens will be treated in the same way when they commit wrongdoings. Nobody is 'above the law': penalties cannot be handed out in an arbitrary manner and the punishments meted out for similar crimes should be the same regardless of who has committed them. This suggests that the law is applied dispassionately and is not subject to the biases and prejudices of those who enforce it. Additionally, all citizens should be aware of the contents of the law. The rule of law, therefore, provides a powerful safeguard to the citizen against arbitrary actions committed by the state and its officials, and is best guaranteed by a judiciary which is independent of the other branches of government.

This principle may be grounded in common law (which was historically the situation in Britain) or it may be incorporated into a codified constitution, as is the case in America.

Although many of the requirements embodied in the principle of the rule of law constitute practices which are widely adhered to in liberal democracies, most liberal democratic states deviate from the strict application of the rule of law. Factors including social background, financial means, class, race or gender may play an influential part in determining whether a citizen who transgresses the law is proceeded against by the state and may also have a major bearing on the outcome of any trial. Additionally, governments may deviate from strict application of the rule of law when emergencies occur.

Equality

Initially, equality sought to remove the privileges enjoyed by certain groups within society so that all of its members were able to lead their lives without impediments being placed upon them derived from factors such as birth, race, gender or religion. This is termed formal equality and is based on views such as the assertion in the American Declaration of Independence (1776) that 'all men are created equal'. This perception of a shared common humanity underpinned the extension of civic rights to all members of society. These included the rule of law (which emphasized equality of all citizens before the law) and reforms such as the abolition of slavery and the removal of restrictions to voting, thus providing for universal male and female enfranchisement.

Although formal equality removed the unfair disadvantages operating against some citizens, it did not tackle the underlying social or economic factors which might enable some members of society to achieve more than others. Other forms of equality have addressed this issue. Social equality is especially concerned with improving the status and self-esteem of traditionally disadvantaged groups in society. Equality of opportunity has underpinned reforms to aid materially the poorer and weaker members of society. This can be achieved by some measure of redistribution of wealth which in the United Kingdom gave rise to the Welfare State or by measures (including equal opportunities and affirmative action programmes) designed to help disadvantaged groups (including women, racial minorities and persons with physical handicaps) who have experienced discrimination in areas such as employment opportunities, pay and housing allocation.

Some socialists favour equality of outcome, which seeks a common level of attainment regardless of an individual's background, personal circumstances or the position in society which they occupy. This may entail a levelling-out process whereby some members of society are penalized in order to ensure social equality. The abolition of wage differentials (so that all persons were paid the same wage regardless of the job they performed) would be one way to secure equality of outcome.

2

liberal democracy

The United Kingdom and the United States of America have liberal democratic political systems. But what does this term mean?

In this chapter we will define the key characteristics of a liberal democratic political system, contrasting this with alternatives that exist in other parts of the world.

One of the key characteristics of a liberal democratic political system is that members of the general public ('citizens') have the ability to shape the way in which they are governed – in particular, which people should govern them and what policies they should carry out. They may do this through elections (which are held regularly to decide who should hold public office) or through other devices such as opinion polls and referendums.

A political system consists of the formal and informal processes through which demands are put forward and decisions are made.

Liberal democratic political systems

Several forms of political system exist throughout the world, a key distinction concerning the allocation of power. A liberal democratic political system is one whose actions reflect the will of the people (or at least the majority of them). In these countries, the public possesses the ability to make demands through a number of channels, which include political parties, pressure groups, the media, elections and extra-parliamentary political action. The suggestions which are put forward in this manner are key aspects of the agenda for the consideration of the formal institutions of government (the legislature, judiciary, executive and bureaucracy) which may also put forward policy proposals of their own. These institutions determine whether to act on demands which are presented to them and if so through what means. Their actions may involve repealing contentious legislation, enacting new laws or taking policy or budgetary decisions.

Popular consent in liberal democratic political systems is secured through representation: liberal (or, as it is sometimes referred to, representative) democracy entails a small group of people taking political decisions on behalf of all the citizens who live in a particular country. Those who exercise this responsibility do so with the consent of the citizens and govern in their name. However, their right to take decisions depends on popular approval and may be withdrawn should they lose the support of the population to whom they are accountable for their actions. In these cases, citizens reclaim the political power they have ceded and reallocate the responsibility for government elsewhere. Elections, which provide a genuine opportunity to exert popular choice over the actions and personnel of government, are thus an essential aspect of liberal democracies. This requires all adults having the right to vote, the regular holding of elections and political parties being able to compete openly for power.

There are wide variations in the political structures which exist within liberal democratic political systems. A major distinction is between those (such as America) that have presidential systems of government and those (such as the United Kingdom) that have parliamentary systems. In some, the executive branch of government tends to be derived from one political party but in others it is drawn from a coalition of parties, perhaps making for a more consensual style of government.

Accountability

Accountability (which is often referred to as responsibility) denotes that an individual or organization to whom power has been delegated is required to submit to the scrutiny of another body or bodies to answer for the actions which have been undertaken. Additionally, the body or bodies to whom the organization or individual is answerable possesses sanctions which can be used in the event of actions being undertaken which are deemed to be unacceptable.

There are two forms of accountability. The individual or organization may have to seek prior permission before taking actions. Alternatively, accountability may entail an individual or organization being free to take actions but required to report what has been done to another body. This is termed *ex post facto* accountability.

In liberal democratic political systems, governments are accountable to the electorate. While in office they may take decisions but the electorate has the ultimate ability to remove them from power at a national election if they disapprove of what has been performed. Elections are thus an essential aspect of liberal democracy which enable the public to exert influence over the legislative and executive branches of government and hold them accountable for their actions. Effective accountability also requires that citizens are in possession of information by which to judge the activities undertaken by public officials. Many liberal democracies provide for this through freedom of information legislation enabling public access to official documents.

Additionally, governments in liberal democratic political systems are accountable to legislatures. They may be required to submit their policies to the scrutiny of legislative bodies, and in parliamentary forms of government, such as that in the United Kingdom, legislatures possess the ability to remove the government by passing a vote of 'no confidence' in it.

Communist and totalitarian political systems

Communist political systems (sometimes referred to as socialist democracies) are political systems based on the ideas of Karl Marx. The most notable feature of communist states is the paramount position of an official socialist ideology and the domination or total monopolization of political affairs by the official Communist Party, whose leading members exert control over institutions such as trade unions, the media and the military and over key state-provided services such as education. Considerable differences exist between them although, in general, these countries are characterized by the existence of little or no private property ownership, a planned economy (which is viewed as essential to achieving equality and classlessness) and a comprehensive welfare state. Communist states include the former Soviet Union and its East European satellite neighbours, but following the 'collapse of communism' in Eastern Europe between 1989–91, is now confined to a smaller number of countries which include the People's Republic of China, Vietnam, Cuba and North Korea.

Totalitarian political systems are those in which the state controls every aspect of the political, social, cultural and economic life of its citizens. It is governed by a ruling elite whose power is based upon ideological control which is exerted over the masses, underpinned by the use of coercive methods. Civil liberties, human rights and the ability of citizens to participate in decision making are very limited, if not totally absent, in such societies. The term 'authoritarian' applies to societies which are also governed by an elite with considerable power, although this is not always exerted over every aspect of civil life as is the case with totalitarianism.

The ideology which is found in totalitarian societies is subject to wide variation. Communist political systems exhibit totalitarian characteristics as they are totally under the control of the Communist Party. Other totalitarian regimes may be dominated by the ideology of fascism, in which only one political party is permitted to exist and representative institutions such as directly elected legislatures are typically absent. Regimes of this nature may also be based upon a religious ideology. These are termed 'theocracies', a word that literally means 'rule by God'. A main feature of theocratic government is its intolerance of viewpoints other than those of the dominant religious sect. Religion or faith plays a dominant role in countries with this form of government: for example, in Iran the president and legislature (which are elected) are subject to the supervision and direction of the clerics.

Totalitarian regimes differ from oligarchic ones. An oligarchy is a political system in which power is held by a small group of persons who govern in their own interests rather than seeking to advance a political ideology. These interests may be economic or may consist of the desire to wield power. As with totalitarian regimes, few political freedoms exist in oligarchic regimes since the general public is not allowed to play any part in politics. They are frequently characterized by brutality and coercion meted out by the police or military who exercise a prominent role in civil affairs. Oligarchies embrace a wide variety of political arrangements including military dictatorships and one-party states, and are typically found in less-developed countries.

Electoral procedures and liberal democracies

Citizens in liberal democracies enjoy a wide range of civil and political liberties. These include entitlements such as the freedoms of expression, movement and association and the existence of an impartial judicial system and freedom from arbitrary arrest. Of particular importance, however, are the procedures that determine how we choose our representatives.

Liberal democracies require mechanisms whereby the general public can exercise choice over who will represent them and also dismiss such persons if they feel that policies lacking popular support are being pursued. This suggests that elections are essential to the operations of liberal democratic political systems. However, elections are not confined to liberal democracies. Countries with alternative political systems may also utilize them. An essential characteristic, therefore, of elections in liberal democracies is that these contests should provide a genuine opportunity to exert popular choice over the personnel and policies of government.

Opinion polls

Opinion polls may be utilized to ascertain public feelings on particular issues. The findings of polls can then be incorporated into the policy proposals put forward by political parties. They are especially prominent in election campaigns. They are used to assess the views of voters on particular issues, which may encourage parties to adjust the emphasis of their campaigns (or the content of their policy) to match the popular mood. They are also employed to investigate the outcome of elections by asking voters who they intend to support. The belief that this activity does not merely indicate public feelings but may actually influence voting behaviour (for example, by creating a bandwagon effect for the party judged by the polls to be in the lead) has prompted countries such as France and Italy to ban the publication of poll results close to the actual contest.

Referendum

Advantages of a referendum

Direct democracy

A referendum permits mass public involvement in public policy making. We term this 'direct democracy'. There are various forms of referendum. They may entail the public being given the opportunity to approve a proposed course of action before it is implemented or to express their views on actions previously undertaken by a government. In America the referendum is frequently used in state government. A widely used version is the petition referendum which enables a predetermined number of signatories to suspend the operation of a law passed by the state legislature, which is then placed before the public at a future state election.

A referendum avoids the dangers of public office holders not accurately reflecting public opinion by enabling the citizens themselves to express their approval or disapproval of issues which affect their everyday lives. The power exercised by policy makers over the content of public policy is reduced and they are required to pursue actions which are truly reflective of the views of the public.

Determination of constitutional issues

It is not feasible to suggest that referenda should be held to ascertain the views of the public on every item of public policy. However, they do provide a means whereby major issues (perhaps of considerable constitutional importance) can be resolved. In many European countries referenda were held on membership of the European Union or treaties (such as Maastricht) which were associated with it because of their implications for fundamental matters such as national sovereignty. Of particular significance was the Constitutional Treaty that was designed to provide the EU with a written constitution. The 25 member states were required to ratify it within two years and some countries did this by holding a referendum. The rejection of this constitution by French and Dutch voters in 2005 effectively made it a 'dead duck'. This resulted in the constitution (which would have replaced all earlier EU treaties) being replaced by a treaty (the Treaty of Lisbon) which merely amended the existing treaties of Rome and Maastricht.

Disadvantages

Devalues the role of the legislature

A referendum may devalue the role performed by legislative bodies. In some countries (such as France) they were deliberately introduced to weaken the power of parliament. Although they can be reconciled with the concept of parliamentary sovereignty when they are consultative and do not require the legislature to undertake a particular course of action, it is difficult to ignore the outcome of a popular vote even when it does not theoretically tie the hands of public policy makers. Thus the Norwegian parliament announced in advance of the 1972 consultative referendum on entry into the European Economic Community that its outcome would determine the country's stance on this issue.

Unequal competition

Competing groups in a referendum do not necessarily possess equality in the resources which they have at their disposal and this may give one side an unfair advantage over the other in putting its case across to the electorate. This problem is accentuated if the government contributes to the financing of one side's campaign, as occurred in the early stages of the 1995 Irish referendum on divorce.

Complexity of issues

The general public may be unable to understand the complexities of the issues which are the subject of a referendum. This may mean that the level of public participation is low or that the result is swayed by factors other than the issue which is placed before the voters for their consideration. For example, the September 2000 referendum in Denmark to reject entry into the single European currency, the euro, was determined more by arguments about the erosion of national identity and independence than by the economic arguments related to joining the euro.

Underlying motives may not be progressive

We should also observe that a referendum is not always a progressive measure designed to enhance the ability of the public to play a meaningful role in policy making. Dictators may use them instead of representative institutions such as a parliament, asserting that these bodies are unnecessary since the public are directly consulted on government policy. The use of referenda by

Germany's Nazi government (1933–45) resulted in the 1949 West German Constitution prohibiting their future use.

'Mob rule'

A referendum may facilitate the tyranny of the majority with minority interests being sacrificed at the behest of mob rule. This may mean that political issues are resolved by orchestrated hysteria rather than through a calm reflection on the issues which are involved.

Low turnout

Public interest in a referendum is not always high and is affected by factors which include the extent to which established political parties are able to agree on a stance to be adopted and campaign for this. Some countries which utilize referenda have a requirement that turnout should reach a stipulated figure in order for reforms to be initiated. This seeks to prevent minorities securing control of the political agenda. In Portugal, for example, a turnout of 50 per cent of the electorate is required for a referendum to have binding authority.

3

political ideologies

The actions that are undertaken by politicians when they hold political office are guided by a body of views and opinions that consist of their core values. These core values are referred to as 'political ideologies'. A number of different political ideologies exist within liberal democratic countries, and throughout the world in general.

This aim of this chapter is thus to define the term 'political ideology' and to provide a very brief discussion of the main political ideologies that are found throughout the world. This will enable you to compare and contrast the approaches that different political ideologies propose should form the basis of political action. The ideologies that are discussed are:

* Anarchism
* Communism
* Socialism
* Social democracy
* Liberalism
* Conservatism
* Fascism

In liberal democracies, political parties seek to secure support from voters by putting forward competing ideologies in election contests.

Definition

Ideology is commonly defined as the principles which motivate political parties, in particular providing a vision of the society they wish to create. Ideology thus serves as a unifying force between party leaders and supporters: all are spiritually united in the promotion of a common cause.

The political spectrum

The various political ideologies are grouped under the broad headings of 'left', 'right' and 'centre'. The right consists of fascism and conservatism, the centre consists of liberalism and social democracy and the left comprises socialism, communism and anarchism. Anarchism is located on the far left of the political spectrum and fascism is on the far right. This terminology was derived from the French Revolution in the late eighteenth century: the left was associated with revolution while the right was identified with reaction.

The terms 'right', 'left' and 'centre' lack precise definition but are used broadly to indicate the stances which the different ideologies adopt towards political, economic and social change. Historically, the right opposed this, preferring tradition and the established order of the past. The left endorsed change as a necessary development which was designed to improve the human condition. The centre was also associated with change, but wished to introduce this gradually within the existing economic and political framework, which the left sought to abolish as a prerequisite to establishing an improved society.

Left-wing political ideologies

A number of political ideologies are identified with the left of the political spectrum. These seek the destruction of capitalism and the establishment of a new social order based upon a fundamental redistribution of wealth, resources and power.

Anarchism

Anarchism literally means 'no rule' and is a form of socialism which rejects conventional forms of government on the basis that they impose restraints on individuals without their express consent having been given. Accordingly, anarchists urge the abolition of the state and all forms of political authority, especially the machinery of law and order (which they view as the basis of oppression, providing for the exercise of power by some members of society over others). Most anarchists deem violence as the necessary means to tear down the state.

Anarchists assert that government is an unnecessary evil since social order will develop naturally. Co-operation will be founded upon the self-interest of individuals and regulated by their common sense and willingness to resolve problems rationally. They assert that traditional forms of government, far from promoting harmony, are the root cause of social conflict. Private ownership of property, which is a key aspect of capitalist society, is regarded as a major source of this friction.

Communism

Communism (sometimes referred to as socialist democracy) is a political system based on the ideas of Karl Marx. According to Marxist theory, communism occurs following the overthrow of capitalism and after an intermediary phase (referred to as socialism) in which the Communist Party functions as the vanguard of the proletariat, ruling on their behalf and paving the way for the eventual establishment of communism. This is characterized by the abolition of private property and class divisions and the creation of equality in which citizens live in co-operation and harmony. In this situation the state becomes unnecessary and will 'wither away'.

States which have called themselves 'communist' have not achieved the ideal situation referred to by Marx. Considerable differences existed between them (especially the former USSR and China, whose approach to issues such as social equality was dissimilar) although in general, these countries were characterized by the existence of little or no private property ownership, a planned economy (which was viewed as essential to achieving equality and classlessness) and a comprehensive welfare state.

The most notable feature of communist states is the paramount position of an official socialist ideology and the domination or total monopolization of political affairs by the official Communist Party. As the massacre of opponents to the communist regime in China at Tiananmen Square in 1989 evidenced, dissent is not encouraged in communist states. The control which the Communist Party exerts over government means that the judiciary is less able to defend civil and political liberties than is the case in liberal democratic political systems.

Communist states included the former Soviet Union and its East European satellite neighbours but, following the 'collapse of communism' in Eastern Europe between 1989–91, communism is now confined to a smaller number of countries which include the People's Republic of China, Vietnam, Cuba and North Korea.

Socialism

Socialism arose in reaction to the exploitive nature of capitalism. It rejects a society in which inequalities in the distribution of wealth and political power result in social injustice and is committed to the ideal of equality. Socialists seek a society in which co-operation and fraternity replace the divisions based on class lines which characterize capitalist societies. There is, however, considerable disagreement concerning both the nature of an egalitarian society and how it would be created. These stem from the diverse traditions embraced by socialism.

The roots of socialism include the economic theories of David Ricardo (who suggested that the interests of capital and labour were opposed), the reforming activities of Robert Owen (who advocated the ownership of the means of production by small groups of producers organized into societies based upon the spirit of co-operation), the Christian impulse (which was relevant to socialism through its concern for the poor and the early experiences of Christians living in a society in which property was held in common) and the writings of Karl Marx and Friedrich Engels who asserted that inequality was rooted in private property ownership and the class system which derived from this.

The varied impulses which influenced socialism explain the differences within it. A key division is between fundamentalist and reformist socialism (or social democracy). Fundamentalist socialists believe that state control of all means of production is indispensable to the creation of an egalitarian society and is thus viewed as their main political objective. They reject the free market and instead have historically endorsed the centralized planning of the economy and the nationalization (or 'socialization' as it is termed in America) of key industries to achieve this goal. Reformist (or revisionist) socialists, however, believe that an egalitarian society can be created by reforming the capitalist system rather than abolishing it. This version of socialism is commonly referred to as social democracy. This has resulted in what is termed a mixed economy. Central economic planning has typically been used to supplement the workings of the free market rather than seeking to replace it.

The centre and centre-left of the political spectrum

This section outlines the key aspects of liberalism and social democracy, which are identified with the centre-left and centre of the political spectrum. The parties based on these ideologies promote social, economic and political change, which they wish to achieve through the ballot box rather than through revolution.

Social democracy

Social democracy rests within the reformist (or revisionist) tradition of socialism. It suggests that social inequalities can be addressed by an enhanced level of state intervention within the existing structure of the capitalist economic system. The influence of social democracy was increased after 1945 when capitalism was seen to be bringing many benefits to working-class people (such as a rising standard of living and social mobility) in a number of countries, which in turn tended to reduce the hostility between the social classes.

Lord John Maynard Keynes was especially influential in the development of social democratic politics. He argued that a market economy subject to an enhanced degree of state intervention to manage demand could provide an effective solution to the problem of unemployment. His policy of demand management was adopted by a number of socialist parties as an alternative to state control of the economy.

Social democracy also sought to remove social problems affecting the poorer members of society through the establishment of a welfare state. This was a mechanism to provide for the redistribution of wealth within society, since the Welfare State would be financed by public money obtained through the taxation of income, so that the rich would contribute towards addressing the health and welfare needs of the poor. Social democracy was also associated with other policies designed to improve the access of poorer members of society to a range of services such as housing and education.

Liberalism

Modern liberalism emerged from the fight for religious freedom waged in late sixteenth- and seventeenth-century Western Europe. Liberal theorists argued that the social order was a compact (or contract) voluntarily entered into by those who were party to it rather than being a structure handed down by God. Social contract theory was developed by liberal theorists such as Thomas Hobbes and John Locke. The belief that government emerged as the result of rational choice made by those who subsequently accorded their consent to its operations ensured that the rights of the individual were prominent concerns of liberal philosophers. The people were viewed as the ultimate source of political power and government was legitimate only while it operated with their consent.

As a political doctrine, liberalism emphasized individualism and asserted that human beings should exercise the maximum possible freedom consistent with others being able to enjoy similar liberty.

They sought to advance this belief through their support for limited government and their opposition to the intervention of the state in the everyday lives of its citizens, arguing that this would dehumanize individuals since they were not required to take responsibility for their own welfare but instead became reliant on others, whom they could blame if personal misfortunes befell them. As an economic doctrine, liberalism was traditionally associated with the free market, laissez-faire capitalism and free trade.

Right-wing political ideologies

This section discusses the main aspects of ideologies on the right of the political spectrum.

Conservatism

The essence of conservative ideology is scepticism towards change and a disinclination to support reform unless this prevents more radical reforms from being implemented. The desire to 'retain things as they are' is especially concerned with what are deemed to be the key institutions and values on which society is based. These include support for private property ownership. This results in opposition to any form of social (including moral) upheaval, support for firm (but not despotic) government and a belief that political institutions should evolve naturally rather than being artificially constructed from an abstract theory or blueprint. Conservatism rejects the goal of equality achieved by social engineering, believing that the differences which exist between people are natural and should not be tampered with. Conservatism is often equated with nationalistic sentiments, seeking to safeguard domestic values and way of life against foreign incursions.

Conservative thought developed in the eighteenth century and was especially influenced by the events of the French Revolution. Conservatism in the United Kingdom was considerably influenced by *Reflexions on the Revolution in France*, written by Edmund Burke in 1792. Although he had initially been sympathetic to the French

Revolution, he subsequently turned against it when the scale of the destruction of the established order became apparent. He explained this alteration in the direction of his thought by providing a summary of the 'British way', which constituted a classic statement of conservatism. He argued that an Englishman's freedom was a national inheritance which was most effectively secured by a government that balanced democracy, aristocracy and monarchy. His defence of traditions and institutions was coupled with the advocacy of evolutionary change. He accepted that change would sometimes be necessary, but advocated that this should be minimal and should seek to preserve as much of the old as was possible.

New right

The term 'new right' refers to a body of ideas that underpinned the policies pursued by a number of conservative parties in the 1980s, most notably in governments led by Margaret Thatcher in the United Kingdom and Ronald Reagan in America.

New right policies were based on two specific traditions. The first of these was termed 'neo-liberalism'. This version of economic liberalism was rooted in classical liberal ideas and sought to reduce the activities of the state, whose frontiers would be 'rolled back' by the application of policies such as privatization and reduced levels of government spending on functions such as welfare provision. This aspect of new right thinking voiced support for private enterprise and the free market and led to Keynesian economics (which regarded unemployment as the key problem to be addressed by economic policy) being replaced by alternative economic methods such as monetarism, which identified inflation as the main social evil. This resulted in policies that included controlling the money supply and keeping a tight rein on interest rates. It was argued that government intervention in the economy led to inefficiency, but that economic growth, employment, productivity and widespread prosperity would be secured if it ceased its attempts to regulate wages and prices.

The second basis of new right thinking was termed 'neo-conservatism'. This emerged in America in the 1960s and was endorsed primarily by liberals who were disillusioned by the inability of government action to solve social problems. It entailed a number of ideas which included social authoritarianism. This asserted that contemporary social problems such as crime, disorder, hooliganism, indiscipline among young people and moral decay were caused by the decline of 'traditional' values, which had been replaced by permissive attitudes and disrespect for authority. Many neo-conservatives apportioned the blame for these problems to the lack of commitment by immigrants to a country's established cultural values. It endorsed a 'law and order' response to social problems and demanded a return to traditional forms of authority such as the family.

Fascism

Fascism is a political ideology on the right of the political spectrum which, although lacking a coherent body of beliefs, shares certain important features. These include opposition to communism, Marxism and liberalism (especially individualism, which fascists advocate should occupy a position subordinate to the national community). Fascism also opposes the operations of liberal democracy, which it seeks to replace with a totalitarian political system in which there is only one party and, ideally, the complete identity of this party with the state. One consequence of this is that civil and political liberties are absent in fascist states.

Fascist parties utilize action and violence as key political tactics, especially when seeking to secure power, and they stress the importance of firm leadership to solve a nation's problems. They also emphasize the importance of nation and race, the consequences of which included a desire for territorial expansion and the practice of racism and genocide.

4

elections and electoral systems

Elections perform a crucial role in liberal democratic political systems. They enable us to exercise a choice over who should represent us in institutions such as the House of Commons, the American Congress or local government.

In this chapter we will start by considering the significance of elections – the role they perform in the conduct of politics. We shall then move on to consider the mechanisms that enable us to select persons to represent us. These mechanisms are referred to as 'electoral systems' and a wide variety exist within liberal democracies. In this chapter we will consider the main ones:

* the first-past-the-post electoral system
* proportional representation
* the additional member system (which blends aspects of both of the above two electoral systems).

We will discuss the main features of these electoral systems and consider their respective strengths and weaknesses.

The significance of elections

Those of us who live in liberal democracies will periodically be invited to vote. Elections are the mechanism whereby citizens are provided with the opportunity to select persons to take political decisions on their behalf. They enable public participation in key activities which include selecting the personnel of government and determining the content of public policy.

Elections further constitute the process whereby public office holders can be made to account for their activities to the general public. Governments that lose the backing of public opinion will be replaced by representatives drawn from another political party at the next round of elections.

However there is no one voting system used by all liberal democracies to elect candidates to a public office. Several different electoral systems are found across the world, all of which possess strengths and weaknesses which we consider below in more detail.

The first-past-the-post electoral system and its variants

The first-past-the-post system is used in countries including the UK, the United States, Canada and India.

Under this system, to be elected to a public office it is necessary for a candidate to secure more votes than the person who comes second. But there is no requirement that the winning candidate should secure an overall majority of the votes cast in an election.

Elsewhere, systems of election have been devised that seek to adjust the workings of the first-past-the-post system. These are the second ballot and the alternative vote. Neither of these constitutes a system of proportional representation although they do attempt to put right some of the injustices which may arise under the first-past-the-post system.

The second ballot

The second ballot is used in France, both for legislative and presidential elections. The process is a two-stage affair. It is necessary for a candidate to obtain an overall majority of votes cast in the first-round election in order to secure election to public office. In other words, if 50,000 people voted in a constituency, it would be necessary for a candidate to secure 25,001 votes to be elected. If no candidate obtains this required figure, a second-round election is held and the candidate who wins most votes is elected. This system seeks to ensure that the winning candidate gets the endorsement of a majority of the electors who cast their votes in the second election.

The alternative vote

The alternative vote is used in Ireland for presidential elections and for by-elections to the lower house, the *Dáil*. It is also used to select members for the Australian House of Representatives. As with the second ballot, a candidate cannot be elected without obtaining majority support from the electorate (namely 50 per cent + 1 of the votes cast). Unlike the second ballot, however, there is no second election.

Voters number candidates in order of preference. If, when these votes are counted, no candidate possesses an overall majority, the candidate with least first-preference votes is eliminated and these are redistributed to the candidate placed second on that candidate's ballot paper. This process is repeated until a candidate has an overall majority composed of his or her first preference votes coupled with the redistributed votes of candidates who have been eliminated.

Proportional representation

Proportional representation indicates an objective rather than a specific method of election. It seeks to guarantee that the wishes of the electorate are arithmetically reflected in the composition of public bodies such as legislatures and local authorities. This is achieved by ensuring that parties are represented according to the level of popular support they enjoy at an election contest. Various forms of proportional representation are used widely in countries within the European Union. This section will consider two of these – the single transferable vote and the party list system.

The single transferable vote

When used for elections to legislatures, the single transferable vote requires a country to be divided into a number of multi-member constituencies (that is, constituencies which return more than one member to the legislative body). When electors cast their votes, they are required to number candidates in order of preference. They may indicate a preference for as many, or as few, candidates as they wish. To be elected a candidate has to secure a quota of votes, calculated by this formula:

$$\frac{\text{total number of votes cast in the constituency}}{\text{total number of seats to be filled} + 1}$$

The party list system

The other main system of proportional representation is the party list system. Its main objective is to ensure that parties are represented in legislative bodies in proportion to the votes which were cast for them. Political parties are responsible for drawing up lists of candidates which may be compiled on a national or on a regional basis.

There are several versions of the party list system. In a very simplistic form (in what is termed a 'closed party list') candidates are ranked in order of preference by political parties. When the votes are counted, a party's representation in the legislative body arithmetically reflects the proportion of votes which it obtained. Thus a party which obtained 20 per cent of the total national poll would be entitled to 20 per cent of the seats in the legislative chamber. If the chamber contained 300 members, this party would be entitled to fill 60 places. The actual nominees would be those numbered 1–60 on that party's list.

The additional member system

The additional (or mixed-) member system of election blends the first-past-the-post system with proportional representation. This mixed system is used in Germany and under this country's additional member system, electors have two votes in parliamentary elections. The first (*Erststimme*) is for a constituency candidate, elected under the first-past-the-post system for each of the country's 299 single-member constituencies. The second (*Zweitstimme*) is for a party list drawn up in each state (or Land).

This system provides for the proportional allocation of seats in the *Bundestag*.

The first-past-the-post electoral system analysed

Strengths

The main strengths of this system are:

* **Easy to understand.** The system is relatively easy to understand. Voting is a simple process and it is easy to see how the result is arrived at. The winner takes all.
* **Executive strength.** The failure of this system to ensure that the composition of the legislature arithmetically reflects the way in which a nation has voted often benefits the party winning most votes nationally. This is of particular importance in parliamentary systems of government such as the UK where the executive is drawn from the legislature, since it may provide the executive with a large majority, thereby enhancing its ability to govern.
* **An aid to party unity.** The manner in which this system treats minorities may serve as an inducement for parties either to remain united or to form electoral alliances in order to secure political power. This is a particular

advantage in countries with parliamentary forms of government since a party's support within the legislature is likely to be durable.

* **Enhancement of the link between the citizens and legislators.** The first-past-the-post system may strengthen the relationship between members of the legislative branch of government and their constituents. In the UK, the House of Commons is composed of members elected from 650 single-member constituencies, which aids the development of a close relationship between individual legislators and their constituents. This may also enhance the extent to which legislators can be held accountable for their actions.

Weaknesses

The first-past-the-post electoral system has a number of weaknesses.

* **Distortion of public opinion.** A main problem with the first-past-the-post system is that it distorts public opinion by failing to ensure that the wishes of the electorate are arithmetically reflected in the composition of the legislative or executive branches of government. This may thus result in public policy being out of line with the views or wishes of the majority of the general public.

* **Unfair treatment of minority parties.** A second problem arising from the operations of the first-past-the-post system is the manner in which it treats minority parties. In the UK, the Liberal Party/Liberal Democrats have, for much of the last century, been under-represented in parliament as the electoral system has failed to translate that party's national vote into seats within the legislature. Although this party has fared better in general elections held since 1997 than in previous contests (as its support became concentrated in certain areas rather than being evenly spread across the country), its share of the national poll in 2010 (23 per cent) entitled it to 149 seats rather than the 57 it actually won.

* **Disincentive to voter participation.** A further problem with the first-past-the-post system is that it may discourage voter participation. Areas may be considered 'safe' political territory for one party or another and this may discourage opponents of that party from voting on the grounds that if they do so their vote is effectively 'wasted'.
* **The downplaying of ideology.** The first-past-the-post system may promote the conduct of politics within the confines of a two-party system. However, this may result in ideology becoming diluted, obscured or played down in order for the parties to serve as vehicles capable of attracting a wide range of political opinions. The absence of a distinct identity may result in voters becoming disinterested in the conduct of politics. The consequence of this is low turnouts in elections and the utilization of alternative ways (such as pressure group activity and various forms of direct action) of bringing about political change.

Attainment of the benefits of the first-past-the-post system

We must finally analyse whether the theoretical advantages of the first-past-the-post system are actually realized in practice.

In the UK, the executive branch of government comes from the majority party in the legislative body. However, strong governments (in the sense of the executive having a large parliamentary majority and thus being in a position to ensure the enactment of its election manifesto) have not been a consistent feature of post-war politics. Eighteen general elections have been held between 1945 and 2010: in six of these (1950, 1951, 1964, February 1974, October 1974 and 1992) governments were returned with a relatively small majority and in two cases (February 1974 and 2010) a 'hung parliament' (in which no single party possessed an overall majority of votes in the new House of Commons) was produced. Governments in this position cannot guarantee to stay in office and carry out their policies.

Advantages

The main advantage of proportional representation is that the system addresses many of the defects of the first-past-the-post system. It ensures that minorities are fairly treated. Legislative bodies throughout Europe contain members drawn from parties such as the Greens and thus provide an inducement for such groups to operate within the conventional political system rather than engage in extra-parliamentary political activity.

Proportional representation may also induce parties to co-operate (especially in cases where the executive is drawn from the legislative body) and this may, in turn, divert politics away from extremes.

Disadvantages

Representation given to political extremists

Proportional representation may facilitate the representation of the political extremes, which, once established within a legislative body, gain respectability and may enjoy a growth in their support. Some countries which use this system seek to guard against this problem by imposing a requirement that a party needs to secure a minimum threshold of support in order to secure the benefits of proportional representation. In Denmark this figure is 2 per cent of the national vote, in Germany 5 per cent (or, alternatively, three seats secured from the constituency contests).

Creation of multi-party systems

The tendency for proportional representation to aid minority parties to obtain representation in legislative bodies may promote the development of a multi-party system. This is of particular significance for those countries with parliamentary forms of government whose executives are drawn from the legislative body. In these cases, multi-party systems may make it difficult for the electorate to determine the composition of the executive or the policies which it pursues. Executives may consist of a coalition of parties are often depicted as being weak and unstable.

Complexity

Critics of proportional representation argue that the system is difficult in the sense that it may not be obvious how the eventual result has been arrived at. This is especially the case with the single transferable vote, which requires a process of redistribution (either of the surplus votes of an elected candidate or of the redundant votes of one who has been eliminated). If the process by which the result is arrived at is not fully understood, the result itself may be deprived of popular legitimacy.

Enhancement of position of party leadership

Proportional representation has been accused of enhancing the power of the party leadership. This is especially the case with the party list system, which may give regional or national party leaders the ability to place candidates in order of preference and thereby improve the chances of loyal party members being elected ahead of those who are regarded as dissentients.

Impact on legislator and constituent relationships

It might be argued that proportional representation weakens the link between legislator and constituent, which in countries such as the UK and America is regarded as a crucial political feature. This problem arises as multi-member constituencies are often large, although this is not a universal feature of proportional representation.

5

parties and party systems

Each liberal democratic country has a number of political parties which contest elections in the hope of achieving power – perhaps control of the national government or of a sub-national unit of government such as a regional assembly or a local authority. In the United Kingdom the main parties are the Conservative and Labour parties and the Liberal Democrats, and in America they consist of the Republicans and Democrats.

In this chapter we will consider the basis upon which political parties are constructed – what interests they were established to represent – and the roles that they play and the advantages that they bring to the conduct of political affairs. We will then move on to discuss the problems that have been encountered by the major political parties in a number of liberal democratic states towards the end of the twentieth century and how these parties have adapted in order to face these challenges.

Objectives and key characteristics

The role of the political parties is to determine the composition of government and the policies that it carries out. To achieve this objective a party may operate independently or it can co-operate with other political parties by participating in coalition governments.

A party possesses a formal structure which involves national leadership and local organization. The main role of the latter is to contest elections and recruit party members. This organization is permanent, although it may be most active at election times. The relationship between a party's leaders and its membership varies quite considerably, especially the extent to which a party's leaders can be held accountable for their actions by its rank-and-file supporters. Policy making is frequently the preserve of the party's national leadership, which may also possess some degree of control over the selection of candidates for public office.

Determinants of party systems

Considerable differences exist within liberal democracies concerning the nature of party systems. Some countries such as the UK, America and New Zealand have relatively few political parties. Scandinavia, however, is characterized by multi-party systems. In order to explain these differences we need to consider what factors influence the development of political parties and party systems.

The basis of party

The degree of homogeneity (that is, uniformity) in a country is an important determinant concerning the formation and development of political parties. Basic divisions within a society might provide the basis of a party. These might include social class, nationalism, religion or race. Any of these factors is capable of providing the basis around which parties are established and subsequently operate. Some form of partisanship in which groups of electors have a strong affinity to a particular political party is crucial to sustain a stable party system.

Selection of political leaders

Parties are responsible for selecting candidates for public office at all levels in the machinery of government. Having selected a candidate, the role of the party is then to secure electoral support for its standard bearer. In particular, a country's national leaders emerge through the structure of political parties. Parties provide the main method for selecting a nation's political elite.

Organization of support for governments

In addition to selecting political leaders, political parties ensure that governments are provided with organized support. This is especially important in parliamentary systems of government in which the executive is drawn from the legislative branch of government. Without the support of party and its accompanying system of party discipline, governments would be subject to the constant fear of defeat. This organization is also adopted by opposition parties, which are thus able to step in and form a government should the incumbent party be defeated. In this sense, parties may also be said to promote political stability by ensuring a smooth transfer of power from one government to another can be accomplished.

Stimulation of popular interest and involvement in political affairs

Political parties also stimulate popular interest and facilitate public participation in political affairs. They perform this function in a number of ways. Parties need to mobilize the electorate in order to win votes and secure the election of their representatives to public office. This requires the party 'selling' itself to the general public. In theory, therefore, a party puts forward its policies and seeks to convince the electorate that these are preferable to those of its opponents. The electorate thus becomes better informed concerning political affairs.

Second, parties enable persons other than a small elite group of public office holders to be involved in political activity. Members of the general public can join political parties and engage in matters such as candidate selection and policy formulation.

Crucially, parties are a mechanism whereby those who hold public office can be made accountable for their actions. Although elections provide the ultimate means to secure the accountability of public office holders, parties may subject these officials to a more regular, day-by-day scrutiny, possessing the sanction of deselecting them as candidates for future elections if they fail to promote party policy.

Promoting national harmony

Political parties simplify the conduct of political affairs and make them more manageable. They transform the demands which are made by individuals and groups into programmes which can be put before the electorate. This is known as the 'aggregation of interests', which involves a process of arbitration in which diverse demands are given a degree of coherence by being incorporated into a party platform or manifesto. One consequence of this is to transform parties into 'broad churches' which seek to maximize their level of support by incorporating the claims of a wide cross-section of society.

Such activity enables parties to promote national harmony. Numerous divisions exist within societies, based among other things on class, religion or race. But to win elections, parties have to appeal to as many voters as possible. In doing this, they may endorse policies and address appeals which transcend social divisions. Thus parties might serve as a source of national unity by conciliating the conflicts between diverse groups in society.

The decline of established parties?

In the UK, 97 per cent of the vote cast in the 1955 general election went to the Labour and Conservative parties. By 1964 this figure had declined to 88 per cent. It was further reduced to

76 per cent in 1992 and 68 per cent in 2005. In France a similar pattern has emerged.

In recent years extreme right-wing parties have benefited from the decline in support for established political parties. Parties which include the *Front National* in France, the Progress Party in Norway, the Danish People's Party, the Swiss People's Party, the Italian Northern League, *Vlaams Blok* in Belgium and the British National Party in the UK have gained considerable support in the late twentieth and early years of the twenty-first centuries.

Below we consider two explanations for the decline in support experienced by established political parties – failures affecting their performance of the traditional functions associated with political parties and social and economic changes that have helped to erode the support traditionally enjoyed by the major parties.

The traditional functions of political parties

A number of problems affecting the manner in which established political parties perform their traditional functions, may have eroded public confidence in their operations.

Political education

Parties may not seek to educate the public in any meaningful manner. Election campaigns may be conducted around trivia rather than key issues. Parties may be more concerned to denigrate an opponent than with an attempt to convince electors of the virtues of their own policies. Or they may decide that the wisest course of political action is to follow public opinion rather than seek to lead it. Thus ideology or policy that is viewed as unpopular might be abandoned by a party in an attempt to win elections.

Popular involvement

We may also question the extent to which parties enable widespread involvement in political affairs. Parties do not always have a mass membership. In America, voters do not 'join' a party as they might, for example, in the UK. However, even in countries where individuals can join a political party they do not always do so in large numbers. French and Irish political parties, for example, lack a tradition of mass membership and tend to be controlled by small elitist groups. Neither are those who do join a party guaranteed a meaningful role in its affairs. The Italian Christian Democrats, for example, have a mass membership but this has little say on matters such as party policy.

Divisiveness

Political parties do not always seek to promote harmony. Some may seek to make political capital by emphasizing existing divisions within society. France's *Front National* has sought to cultivate support by blaming that country's economic and social problems on immigration, especially from North Africa. The scapegoating of racial or religious groups, depicting them as the main cause of a country's problems, is a common tactic of the extreme right and serves to create social tension rather than harmony.

Self-interest

The role of parties as dispensers of patronage may result in accusations that they are mainly concerned to award 'jobs for the boys'. This may result in popular disenchantment with the conduct of political affairs, with politics being associated with the furtherance of self-interest rather than with service to the nation.

Political parties and social and economic change

In addition to problems affecting the way in which political parties discharge their traditional functions, social and economic changes in contemporary society have eroded the support enjoyed by the established political parties.

Fundamental changes to a country's economic or social structure might have a significant effect on its political parties. For example, the decline in jobs in the French steel, coal and shipbuilding industries has been cited as one explanation for the reduced support for the Communist Party. Immigration may influence the growth of racist political parties. Below we consider social and economic changes that have contributed to the loss of support for the major political parties.

Dealignment

There are two aspects of dealignment – partisan dealignment and class dealignment.

Partisan dealignment means that a large number of electors either desert the party to which they were traditionally committed or identify with the party which they historically supported far more weakly.

Class dealignment suggests that the historic identity between a political party and a particular social class becomes of reduced significance. In the United Kingdom this might be explained after 1970 by the reduced intensity of class consciousness which arose for a number of reasons, including the increased affluence of the working class (which is termed 'embourgeoisement'), the decline in the number of manual workers and the rise in the service sector of employment.

The twin effects of partisan and class dealignment have two main consequences for the conduct of politics. It results in third parties obtaining increased levels of support, and makes the core support given to established major parties less consistent from one general election to the next. These factors make voting behaviour more volatile.

Realignment

Realignment entails a redefinition of the relationship between political parties and key social groups within society which has a fundamental impact on their relative strength. Partisan and class dealignment, which entail the loosening of traditional bonds attaching individuals and groups to particular parties, may be the prelude to realignment. The formation of new relationships is usually confirmed in what is termed a 'realigning election', which is seen as the start of new patterns of political behaviour.

In America, the victories of Ronald Reagan in 1980 and 1984 were based on the existence of a new coalition. The preference of white male voters in the southern states of America for the Republican Party indicated a major shift in this group's political affiliation which had taken place earlier in the 1970s.

The continued vitality of established political parties

Although the position of established political parties in many liberal democracies is weaker than was previously the case, it seems likely that they will continue to carry out important roles within liberal democratic political systems. One reason for this is that parties are adaptable and have understood the importance of reform.

Reforms to restore the vitality of parties may take a number of forms. They include attempts to increase the number of citizens joining such organizations. In countries such as America, where local parties have often been controlled by 'bosses', initiatives to increase party membership have sometimes been accompanied by reforms designed to 'democratize' the workings of political parties and ensure that members are able to exercise a greater degree of control over key party affairs, including the selection of candidates and the formulation of policy.

There have been problems associated with such developments. Increasing the membership of local parties has sometimes (although not consistently) resulted in accusations of extremists 'taking over' control of an organization, which in turn makes it difficult for parties to appeal to a wide electoral base in order to win elections. What is termed 'coalition building' in America becomes difficult if a party is associated with extremist issues.

Similar problems beset the UK Labour Party in the early 1980s, which resulted in that party's disastrous showing in the 1983 general election in which it placed a manifesto before the electorate based on left-wing principles. These policies emerged as a result of reforms designed to democratize that organization by giving rank-and-file members a greater role in party affairs, principally the selection of party candidates and the party leader.

6

pressure groups and the media

This chapter will define the term 'pressure group', consider the roles that they perform in political affairs and enable us to differentiate between the different types of pressure groups that operate within liberal democratic countries.

A key aspect of the role of pressure groups is to influence policy-makers and the chapter will discuss the various ways whereby they seek to achieve this influence and the factors which help to determine whether they are successful or not in achieving their objectives. We will also consider the benefits that pressure groups bring to the operations of liberal democratic government and the problems that are posed by their activities.

Pressure groups act as a mechanism through which the public can be involved in political activity. The media may stimulate this activity by acting as a source of information on which political choices can be based. This chapter defines the term 'media' and considers the role that it performs in political affairs.

Pressure groups

A pressure group (which may also be termed an 'interest group' or an 'advocacy group') is an organization with a formal structure which is composed of a number of individuals seeking to further or defend a common cause or interest. These groups operate at all levels of society. For the purposes of our discussion, however, we shall concentrate on those seeking to exert influence over national government policy making either by seeking to promote reform or by attempting to prevent it.

The role of pressure groups

A major concern of pressure groups is to persuade policy makers to consider their views and then to act upon them. This involves inducing policy makers either to adopt a course of action which they did not initially intend to embark upon or to abandon a measure which they had originally decided to introduce. If a group succeeds in getting its views acted upon, it may also become involved in further stages of the policy-making process. Pressure groups may be concerned with the implementation of policy and with monitoring it to ensure that the desired aims are achieved.

Classification of pressure groups

Various ways may be adopted to classify the pressure groups which are to be found within liberal democratic political systems. One method is to differentiate according to the relationship which exists between the objective put forward by the group and its membership. This provides us with two broad categories into which groups might be placed.

Sectional groups

These are groups in which the members have a vested interest in the success of their organization. They stand to benefit materially if the aims of the group are adopted by policy makers.

Such organizations are sometimes referred to as 'interest' or 'economic' groups. The membership of sectional groups tends to be narrow and restrictive, drawn from people with similar backgrounds. In the UK, examples include employers' associations (such as the Confederation of British Industry), professional bodies (such as the British Medical Association) and labour organizations (such as the Transport and General Workers' Union).

Promotional (or cause) groups

These are organizations in which the members are united in support of a cause which does not necessarily benefit them materially. They tend to view the work of the group as a moral concern and their aim is to change social attitudes and values. Membership of promotional groups is open to all who share their objectives: members are typically drawn from a wide range of social or occupational backgrounds and are united solely by their common support for the cause advocated by the organization.

The activities of pressure groups

Pressure groups operate throughout the machinery of government.

The executive branch of government

The relationship between groups and the executive branch of government may be constructed in a number of ways. Some have a permanent relationship with government departments. Members representing a group may be appointed to joint advisory committees, which are mechanisms through which the concerns of a pressure group can be made known to the relevant government department. Alternatively, some pressure groups enjoy regular access to civil servants and they may also be involved in discussions on appointments to bodies which are responsible to a department. Groups in this position are termed 'insider' groups. This denotes the close relationship and regular consultation which some groups enjoy with key members of the policy-making process.

The legislature

There are a number of ways whereby pressure groups may seek to exert influence over the legislature. A major mechanism is that of lobbying. This describes communication between someone other than a citizen acting on his or her own behalf and a government policy maker with the intention of influencing the latter's decisions.

Much lobbying is carried out by pressure groups. Some employ full-time lobbyists to promote their interests while others hire lobbyists on a temporary basis when they wish to advance, or secure the defeat of, legislation that is relevant to their interests. The influence that they are able to exert over policy makers is derived from their being regarded as an important source of information.

Pressure groups may voice their concerns to the legislature through ways other than lobbying. In both the UK and America, investigations conducted by the legislature provide a mechanism for the articulation of group interests, while in Germany the committee system utilized by the *Bundestag* secures pressure group influence over legislation.

The judiciary

Pressure groups may turn to the courts to secure the adoption of their aims, usually by challenging the legality of legislation. This approach was crucial to the American civil rights movement. Organizations such as the National Association for the Advancement of Colored People used this mechanism in their fight against segregation practised by a number of the southern states.

The role of the courts is less prominent in countries such as Britain and New Zealand, where judicial challenge to national legislation is precluded by the concept of parliamentary sovereignty, but pressure groups may utilize the courts and launch test cases or challenge the legality of the way in which the law has been implemented.

Indirect pressure

Pressure groups may also seek to influence the key institutions of government through indirect means.

Political parties

The relationship that exists between pressure groups and political parties may be organizational or financial. Traditionally social democratic parties had close relationships of this nature with trade unions. Although this link has been severed in both Germany and Sweden, leading trade unions remain affiliated to the British Labour Party while the Conservatives receive funding and support from the business sector.

Pressure groups and public opinion

Pressure groups often take their case 'to the streets' and seek to mobilize public support for their objectives. Demonstrations are a frequently used tactic. In doing this they seek to influence policy makers by demonstrating the extent of public support for their views.

The international arena

Pressure groups do not confine their activities to one country but increasingly operate on a world stage. They may be international organizations seeking the universal adoption of standards of behaviour throughout the world. Amnesty International (which is concerned with human rights) is an example of such a body.

Pressure groups have also adapted to the development of supranational governmental organizations. The policy makers of the European Union (principally the Commission and Council of Ministers) are subject to pressure group activity.

International institutions, such as the United Nations Human Rights Committee and the European Court of Justice, have also been used by pressure groups which seek to question the actions undertaken by individual governments.

The extent to which tactics used by pressure groups succeed in influencing policy makers depends on a range of factors which we now consider.

The ability of a group to mobilize support

The level of support enjoyed by a group may be one determinant of its strength. Successful groups need to represent all who adhere to a particular interest or a specific cause. The fragmentation of French labour organizations into a number of competing federations has tended to weaken their influence over policy makers and is in contrast to the organizational unity of business interests (whose trade associations are linked by the umbrella organization, CNPF). The strength of American labour organizations is reduced by the low affiliation rate of workers to trade unions.

Expertise commanded by a group

A further factor that may affect the influence groups exercise over policy making is the expertise which they are able to command. Governments may be reliant upon such bodies for advice on the technical and complex issues that surround much contemporary public policy and may further be reliant on a group's goodwill or support to implement policy.

Resources possessed by a group

The resources which pressure groups are able to command may also determine the success or failure of a group. Economically powerful groups possess the ability to publicize their objectives and also to resist sanctions that may be deployed against them. Employer organizations are often influential for such reasons. By contrast, consumer groups have traditionally suffered from lack of resources which may help to explain their difficulties in securing influence over the actions of policy makers. Some governments, however (such as the French), and supranational bodies (such as the European Union) have contributed towards the funding of pressure groups, which offsets weaknesses that derive from lack of funds.

Sanctions available to a group

The sanctions which an organization is able to deploy may be a factor in its ability to influence policy making. Investment decisions or strikes may be used as weapons by business groups or trade unions to influence the conduct of policy makers. Consumer boycotts may influence the practices of the private sector. Groups involved in the implementation of public policy possess the ability to withhold their co-operation and thus prevent the progress of policies to which they object.

The strengths and weaknesses of pressure group activity

Benefits of pressure groups

Popular involvement in policy making

Pressure groups ensure that the policy-making process is not monopolized by politicians or senior civil servants. The control which they are able to exercise is to some extent offset by the operations of pressure groups. Additionally, these organizations aid the participation of members of the general public in policy making, whose role in political affairs is thus not merely confined to casting a vote in elections.

Political education

The need for pressure groups to 'sell' their case to secure influence may aid the process of public education in political affairs. Groups may need to explain what they believe in and why they endorse the views that they hold. Groups that oppose government policy may engage in activities such as investigative journalism, which results in enhanced scrutiny and popular awareness of government activity.

Promote reform

Pressure groups may raise matters which the major political parties would prefer to ignore either because they do not consider them to be mainstream political issues, which generally dominate election campaigns (such as the economy or law and order), or because they are internally divisive to the parties. The emergence of women's issues and environmental concerns onto the political agenda owed much to the activities of pressure groups.

Put forward minority interests

The workings of liberal democratic political systems may also benefit from the ability of pressure groups to advocate minority opinions or concerns. Liberal democracies tend to pay most heed to majority opinion. There is thus a risk that minorities get ignored. Pressure groups provide a vehicle whereby minorities can articulate their needs and encourage policy makers to pay heed to them.

Disadvantages of pressure groups

Inequality

One problem associated with pressure groups is that all are not given the same degree of attention by policy makers. The influence they are able to command is considerably influenced by factors including the resources at the group's disposal and the relationships they have constructed with government departments.

This situation may result in worthy minority causes making little impact on public policy as they are relatively ignored by bureaucrats, ministers, political parties, the media and public opinion.

Also, the ability of some groups to command considerable economic resources and be in possession of powerful sanctions which they can deploy to further their interests may result in them being in a position not merely to influence but to dominate the policy-making process.

Internal democracy

A further difficulty which we encounter with the workings of pressure groups is the extent to which the opinions or actions of the leadership faithfully reflect the views of the membership. Most pressure groups are not subject to such internal regulation and are thus susceptible to domination by their leaders. In this situation pressure groups fail greatly to extend the degree of popular involvement in policy making.

Methods used to secure influence

Concern has been expressed within liberal democracies regarding the expenditure of money by pressure groups in order to achieve influence. The purposes of such spending may go beyond political education and extend into activities which are perceived to approximate bribery or corruption. Lobbying has been a particular cause of concern and has led some countries to introduce measures to regulate these activities. In America, for example, lobbying activities directed at the federal government are regulated by the 1995 Lobby Disclosure Act.

Undermine the capacity of a government to govern

Pressure groups may embark on activities that disrupt the conduct of civil affairs and make it impossible for the government to govern. An example of this occurred in the UK in 2000 when protesters who objected to the high cost of fuel blockaded oil refineries and stopped the movement of fuel. This action brought the country to a standstill with fuel being moved only to those locations approved by the protesters.

The role of the media in political affairs

The role of pressure groups in stimulating public activity in political affairs is supplemented by work performed by the media. The media consist of mechanisms of communication: historically the media consisted mainly of newspapers, but today they are more diverse and include journals, radio, television and newer means of electronic communication using computer technology. The internet is now a major mechanism of international communication and is widely utilized as a key source of information regarding political affairs and also as a means to organize extra-parliamentary political activities on a global basis – rallies. The media performs two key roles in political affairs.

A source of information

The media are a source of information concerning internal and international events. By reading, listening to or viewing the media, members of the general public are informed about events of which they have no first-hand knowledge and thereby become more politically aware. One advantage of this is that public participation in policy making is facilitated. Public opinion is able to exert pressure on governments over a wide range of matters which, but for the role of the media, would be confined to the knowledge of a relatively small, elite group of rulers.

Scrutiny of government

The media act as a watchdog and scrutinize the activities performed by governments. The electorate has information placed at its disposal with which it can judge the record of governments: in particular the shortcomings or errors committed by individual ministers or by the government as a whole may be exposed. In this manner, the media perform an important function by ensuring that governments can be held effectively accountable to the electorate.

Problems posed by the media

Partisanship

The first problem is that of partisanship. Although in countries such as the UK and Ireland, radio and television are subject to legislation which is designed to prevent programmes favouring one politician or political party at the expense of another, other sections of the media, especially the press, are politically biased: they may support one party which they portray in a favourable light while seeking to belittle its political opponents.

Press bias is primarily effected through analysis: that is, newspapers do not simply report events, but seek to guide the public to a particular interpretation of those occurrences and the manner in which problems might be resolved. One way this is done is by blurring fact and opinion. This results in a story which is slanted towards the political perspective that the newspaper wishes to advance.

Partisanship is not necessarily a problem: if a country possesses a press which is diverse, a relatively wide range of political opinion will be presented. The biases of one newspaper, for example, can be offset by another presenting a totally different report or analysis of the same issue. Most members of the general public, however, do not read a wide range of newspapers and thus secure a balanced view. We tend to be selective in our choice of newspaper and thus may be influenced by the interpretation which it puts forward.

This problem of bias has been compounded by recent developments in the concentration of ownership. In many liberal democracies a number of newspapers are owned by one individual which may restrict the diversity of views expressed in that nation's press. Examples of such 'press barons' include Silvio Berlusconi in Italy, the Springer Group in Germany and Rupert Murdoch whose worldwide interests cover Europe, Asia and (following the acquisition of Direct TV in 2003) North and Latin America.

Selective coverage of events

A second criticism which is sometimes levelled against the media concerns the process by which events are selected for coverage. It is argued that stories which appear in our newspapers or on our television screens are chosen not according to their importance but, rather, by the criterion of 'newsworthiness' applied by media owners or editors. This may mean that stories which are sensational get media coverage at the expense of worthier events which lack such 'glamour'.

This criticism suggests that the media do not fulfil their role of educating the public since they are selective in the information provided and how this is presented. This is especially of concern if media owners or editors concentrate on trivia at the expense of key issues of national or international concern.

Privacy versus the 'right to know'

A third criticism which has been directed against the media is concerned with editorial freedom: should the media be free to publish any story which they believe is of interest to the general public or should limits exist to prevent publication under certain circumstances? Censorship is regarded as anathema to a liberal democratic system of government. However, restrictions on the media exist in all liberal democratic systems of government. For example, it is a requirement that reports should be truthful. Those which are not might be subject to actions for slander or libel. A more contentious restriction concerns state interests. Legislation (such as the United Kingdom's 1989 Official Secrets Act) is designed to protect the state against subversive activities waged by foreign governments.

One difficulty is that state interests are difficult to define precisely. Should the term cover such activities performed by a government in the name of the state which it might find politically embarrassing if revealed to the general public or to world opinion?

Another contentious area is that of individual privacy. The media's watchdog function may involve publishing information which infringes on the personal life of a public figure. Such information may be obtained in dubious ways including the use of telephoto lenses or bugging devices. This reveals an important dilemma: where does the public's 'right to know' stop and a public person's 'right to privacy' begin?

The media and the conduct of politics

In all liberal democracies the media exert a profound influence over the conduct of political affairs.

Television, in particular, has had a number of consequences for the conduct of national elections. This provides candidates with an opportunity to address large audiences and 'head-to-head' televised debates are common in countries with directly elected presidents.

This is especially the case in America, where televised debates between the two main contenders for the office of president were introduced in 1960 (between Richard Nixon and John F. Kennedy) and became a feature of all subsequent contests after 1976. They are organized by the Commission on Presidential Debates.

Even in countries with a parliamentary form of government such as the UK, television has tended to focus attention on party leaders and thus transform general elections into contests for the office of prime minister. In such countries, national elections have become 'presidentialized'. This trend was accentuated in the UK 2010 general election when the leaders of the three main parties took part in a series of three televised debates. Central control over party affairs has also been enhanced by this development, which has also tended to reduce the importance of activities performed by local party members in connection with the election of candidates to public office.

Additionally, television has placed emphasis on presentation: major political events such as campaign rallies are carefully orchestrated so that viewers are presented with an image of a united and enthusiastic party. Leading politicians are carefully schooled in television techniques since the ability to perform professionally on television has become an essential political skill. Advertising companies play an ever-increasing role in 'selling' political parties and their leaders. The danger with such developments is that content may be of secondary importance to what advertisers refer to as 'packaging'.

However, the influence of the media over the conduct of politics is not confined to national elections. The role performed by legislatures may also be adversely affected. Investigative journalism may provide more effective scrutiny of the actions of the executive than a legislator's speeches or questions. An appearance by a legislator in a brief televised interview will reach a wider audience than a speech delivered within the legislature.

Agenda setting

It is argued that the media have the ability to 'set the political agenda': that is, the media may publicize a particular issue in the hope of concentrating the attention of their readers, listeners or viewers on this topic. Whether this is a good or a bad development much depends on the motives that lie behind the media's attempts to influence public perceptions. A beneficial aspect of this activity is that the media may lead public opinion in a progressive direction, perhaps securing action on a social problem which would otherwise have been ignored.

Alternatively, however, the media may be guided by partisan motives. Attention may be directed at an issue in order to secure support for a course of action favoured by their owners or by the political interests which the owners support. This may involve whipping up public hysteria to persuade governments to act in a manner advocated by the media or the interests which lay behind them.

Reinforcement or change?

Agenda setting is, however, only one aspect of media influence. It is sometimes argued that the media have the ability to determine not merely the policies which governments adopt but, more fundamentally, their political complexion. This accusation implies that the media have a significant influence over voting behaviour at election times. There are two basic schools of thought concerning the ability of the media to influence how we vote. The debate centres on the extent to which the media merely reinforce existing political behaviour rather than being able to act as the agent of political change.

Those who argue that the media reinforce existing political activity suggest that the power of the media over politics is limited since most members of the general public have preconceived political opinions. They will either read, listen to or view material which is consistent with these existing ideas or ignore contrary ideas should these be expressed. Further, as the media know the tastes of their clientele, they will cater for these opinions and not run the risk of losing readers, listeners or viewers. The reinforcement theory thus suggests that issues of media bias are of no significant political importance even at election times.

A contrary opinion to the reinforcement theory suggests that the media have a profound influence over political activity such as voting behaviour. It is suggested that many people are unaware of the political biases of the media to which they are subject and may thus be influenced by the manner in which they portray events, especially when such exposure takes place over a long period of time.

However, the extent to which the media influence political affairs is open to debate. It is one social agency among several others (which include the family, the workplace or the neighbourhood) which may affect political conduct. Those without established political views or loyalties (who are described as 'don't knows' in opinion polls) may be most susceptible to media influence.

7

the executive branch of government

This chapter considers the operations of the executive branch of government. It starts by examining the work undertaken by a senior group of politicians (whom we often refer to as the 'government'), distinguishing between parliamentary or presidential systems of government and contrasting the manner in which power is shared within the executive branch of government.

We consider the power that is wielded by the one politician who heads the executive branch of government (who is referred to as the 'chief executive'). These politicians are regarded as the political leaders of their nations. We are especially concerned with how these officials are chosen and what restrictions may limit the power they are able to exercise. We discuss the functions performed by a head of state who may also be the nation's chief executive (as is the case in America) or may be a different person (as in the case in the United Kingdom).

Finally, we consider the role of 'bureaucrats' (or 'civil servants'), and their function in the executive branch of government.

In this and the following chapters we consider the operations of the three branches of government. These consist of the executive, the legislature and the judiciary.

The role and powers of these branches of government and the inter-relationships between them are defined in a country's constitution. Constitutions are of two types – codified (which means that information related to the operations of government, in particular what it can do and what it can't do) are contained in one document. Examples of codified constitutions include the American Constitutions that was drawn up in 1787. Codified constitutions which have a status superior to that or ordinary law and in countries which have them, the courts have the ability to strike down ordinary law that contravenes the constitution through the process of judicial review.

Some countries have uncodfied constitutions. This means that its governing arrangements are contained in a number of different sources. The United Kingdom's constitution is uncodifed and information concerning its government is found in a number of sources that include Acts of Parliament, European law, common law and conventions.

We commence our consideration of government by examining the executive. The work of the executive branch of government is performed by two distinct sets of people. These are politicians and paid, permanent officials, or the 'bureaucracy'. We will begin the discussion by concentrating on the role performed by politicians who give leadership to the executive branch of government.

The role of the executive branch

The political control of a state's affairs is under the direction of a broadly constituted group of political appointees. We usually refer to these as 'the government'. For example, in the UK the government consists of the prime minister, cabinet and junior ministers. In America it is composed of the president and the cabinet. Within liberal democracies, governments tend to be either parliamentary or executive.

In a parliamentary system of government the executive branch of government is drawn from the legislature and is also collectively accountable to this body for its actions. The office of head of state is separate from the chief executive, the latter being the leader of the largest political party (or coalition of parties) commanding support in the legislature, who is called upon by the head of state to form a government. Its tenure in office is dependent on retaining the legislature's support, and chief executives typically possess the ability to recommend the dissolution of the legislature to the head of state which triggers a general election. Countries which have this form of government include the UK and Germany.

In the UK, the prime minister, members of the cabinet and junior ministers are members of parliament (most being drawn from the House of Commons). The government operates with the consent of parliament and especially the House of Commons, which possesses the ultimate sanction, that of passing a motion of 'no confidence' in it which requires it to resign.

A presidential system of government is a political structure in which different personnel compose the executive and legislative branches. The executive branch is elected for a fixed term and also occupies the position of head of state. The legislature has no formal relationship with the executive branch of government other than its ability to remove the president through the process of impeachment, and the president does not have the power to dissolve the legislature and call a general election. This system of government is found in both North and South America.

Presidential powers are limited by the need to secure the legislature's support for certain executive actions. Thus one major problem faced by chief executives is how to mobilize the legislature to secure the attainment of their policy goals.

There are, however, hybrid systems which include elements of parliamentary and presidential systems of government. In Israel, for example, the prime minister has been directly elected since 1996 but is responsible to parliament (the *Knesset*).

Leadership within the government is exercised by a chief executive. This person appoints other members of the government and usually exercises a pre-eminent position within it, being regarded as the nation's 'leader'.

There are broadly two models which describe the manner in which political power is allocated within the executive branch of government. Power may be held by the chief executive alone. This is the case in America where the president is regarded as the main source of power within the executive branch of government. He is separately elected and can thus claim an electoral mandate to initiate recommendations concerning public policy. Alternatively, power may be held by a group of individuals who include the chief executive and other leading members of the government.

The term 'cabinet government' describes this latter situation and is more likely to be found in parliamentary systems of government.

In the United Kingdom, there is a strong tradition of cabinet government. This suggests that political power is shared between the chief executive and other members of the government. Major issues of public policy are discussed by all members of the government as a team, presided over by the prime minister. In recent years, however, the nature of cabinet government in this country has been subject to debates which have questioned the ability of a small group of people to determine major issues of policy. It has been suggested that the United Kingdom's system of government has become 'prime ministerial' or 'presidential'.

How chief executives are chosen

The way in which chief executives are chosen varies widely as the following examples show.

In the UK, the chief executive is the leader of the largest party following a general election. This person is formally appointed as prime minister by the head of state, the monarch.

In Germany, the chief executive, or chancellor, is elected by the *Bundestag* from the ranks of the largest party or coalition of parties following a national election. It also elects a cabinet.

In the United States, the chief executive (the president) is directly elected, although this official is technically chosen by a body termed the 'electoral college'. Elections to choose the American president are organized by the states. Each of these is allocated a number of votes in the electoral college, which comprises the total number of representatives sent by each state to both houses of Congress. There were 538 electoral college votes for the 2004 presidential election. Popular vote determines which candidate wins a particular state and all of that state's electoral college vote is allocated for that victor regardless of the size of his or her winning majority.

The electoral college vote is physically cast in Washington by a slate of electors consisting of party officials chosen by the party whose presidential candidate wins the state. These electors are formally approved by each state legislature and are pledged to support the candidate who won their state (although in only 16 states are individual electors required by state law to cast their votes for that candidate). The votes cast in the electoral college are transmitted to the Senate, which counts them and formally declares the result of the presidential election.

The power of chief executives

It is often assumed that chief executives occupy a dominant position in the political system, from which they are able successfully to advance initiatives designed to achieve their objectives or those of the government they head. In this section we consider the difficulties that chief executives in the United Kingdom and America may encounter when seeking to advance their political aims and which thus serve as constraints on their power.

The UK prime minister

It is frequently asserted that the prime minister possesses considerable control over the conduct of political affairs in the

United Kingdom. However, while there are few formal restraints on this office, the prime minister is subject to a range of informal pressures which may greatly limit that person's power.

Control of parliament

The parliamentary situation may restrict the ability of a prime minister to achieve political objectives. The prime minister is the leader of the majority party in parliament, which means that the chief executive's ability to exercise control over political affairs is potentially greatest when that party has a sizeable majority in the House of Commons. A government with a small, or no, majority may have to rely on members drawn from other parties to sustain it in the regular votes which occur. In this circumstance, the prime minister may have to agree to demands made by other politicians or parties on whom the government is forced to rely.

Unity of the parliamentary party

A prime minister's power may also be affected by the unity of his or her parliamentary party. Internal divisions may exercise considerable influence on the composition of the government and a prime minister may be constrained to ensure that party balance is reflected in its make-up. A disunited parliamentary party may make it difficult for the prime minister to secure the passage of policies through the House of Commons. Discontented members may abstain, vote against their own party or even defect to the opposition. This may increase the government's reliance on other parties to secure parliamentary victory. While a prime minister may seek to quell revolts by threatening to dissolve parliament and hold a general election, this is a double-edged sword and is rarely a credible sanction which can be deployed.

Public opinion

Public opinion may also affect the power of the prime minister. Prime ministers may find it easiest to assert themselves when there is a demonstrable degree of support from the electorate for themselves and the governments which they head. When the level of this support declines (tested in opinion polls, parliamentary by-elections or local government elections) a prime minister is in a weaker position. Accordingly, the ability to manipulate the media is of crucial importance to a contemporary prime minister.

The loss of public support may not necessarily affect the conduct of the prime minister. They can either ignore the loss of support and continue with existing policies or bow to public pressure and make changes in either the personnel or the policy of the government.

The American president

The American Constitution placed the executive branch in the hands of a president who is now directly elected. The president serves a term of four years and may be re-elected on one further occasion. The power exercised by a president depends to some extent on personal choice. Presidents may view themselves as officials who should merely enforce the laws passed by Congress, or they may see themselves as dynamic initiators of public policy. These views are further flavoured by popular opinion.

The belief that American presidents should be strong and assertive in the conduct of public affairs was bolstered by the need for decisive presidential action to cope with the Depression in the 1930s. But this view has subsequently been revised by the perceived failings of strong presidents as revealed by the outcome of the Vietnam War (which was associated with presidential initiative) and the belief that strong executive action could lead to abuse of power, as was evidenced in Watergate and the subsequent forced resignation of President Nixon in 1974. Such factors have tended to make the public suspicious of presidents who wish to exercise dynamic leadership. Their ability to initiate actions was further weakened by the size of the budget deficit, which grew enormously during the Reagan–Bush years (1981–93) and served as a constraint on policies involving state intervention.

However, presidents retain a considerable degree of manoeuvre. They possess a range of formal and informal powers and may also exploit their position as the only national unifying force to secure the attainment of their objectives.

The president's mandate

The mandate that a president obtains in a general election may greatly influence subsequent behaviour. A president may feel it is legitimate to exercise the initiative in public affairs when the outcome of an election provides a clear statement of public support for a stated programme. When the outcome of an election is less clear (for example, the president fails to secure a majority of the popular vote) or it appears that the result was more concerned with the rejection of one candidate than with the popular endorsement of the winner, the president may find it more difficult to promote policy vigorously, especially when this involves initiating radical changes.

Clearly focused policy goals

Presidential success in initiating public policy may be most easily realized when policy goals are clearly focused. This suggests a limited set of key objectives which enable both Congress and public opinion in general to appreciate the president's fundamental concerns. The president's state of the union address provides an opportunity to specify key policy goals.

Relations with Congress

A president's relations with Congress have a fundamental bearing on that official's power. The president (unlike the UK's prime minister) has no direct connection with the legislature and Congress may not be inclined to follow the presidential lead. Congress has become more assertive since the 1970s, which has been to the detriment of presidents seeking to exercise a dominant role in both domestic and foreign affairs.

Theoretically, the party system might secure a degree of support for the president from within Congress, but this does not operate in the same way as it does in the United Kingdom. Changes to the process by which presidential candidates are nominated and the manner in which presidential election campaigns are financed has been to the detriment of the relationship between a president and established party organization. Further, parochialism exerts considerable influence over the conduct of members of Congress. Members of Congress may be more willing to follow the president's lead when they feel this will bring personal political benefits to them, but be inclined to distance themselves from the administration if they feel that association with the president constitutes an electoral liability.

Thus, even when the president's party controls both Houses of Congress, this is no guarantee that all members of that party will support the president on every major policy initiative. However, the position of the president is weaker when the opposition party controls either or both Houses of Congress. A position of 'gridlock' may arise (in which president and Congress refuse to give way on key policy issues) and the majority party may also utilize its control of key congressional committees to vigorously scrutinize the policies pursued by the president by the use of their ability to mount investigations underpinned by the power to subpoena. Opposition control of one or both Houses of Congress was a situation that early post-war Republican presidents frequently had to endure and which President Clinton had to suffer for much of his presidency following the loss of Democrat majorities in both Houses in the November 1994 Congressional elections.

Heads of state

There is considerable variety within liberal democracies concerning the office of head of state. In countries such as the UK, the head of state is a constitutional monarch, whose position is derived from birth. In other countries the head of state is elected. This may be direct election (as is the case in Ireland) or indirect election (as is the case in Italy where the president is elected by a college of 'grand electors', which includes members of both houses of parliament and regional governments). In most liberal democracies, the office of head of state is separate from that of chief executive, although in America the president occupies both roles.

Typically, heads of state appoint chief executives or signify the formal approval of legislation. In most cases these are formal endorsements of decisions that have already been made, but the participation of the head of state to some extent neutralizes the party political dimension of the activity.

The role of the bureaucracy

This aspect of our study concerns the administrative arm of the executive branch of government. Here the work is performed by paid officials whom we term 'bureaucrats'. Many of these are categorized as civil servants. This means that key matters such as recruitment, pay, promotion, grading, dismissal and conditions of work are subject to common regulations which operate throughout the national government within which they work. Such common regulations are enforced centrally by bodies such as the American Office of Personnel Management or the United Kingdom's Civil Service Commission.

Civil servants perform a variety of roles in liberal democratic states, but there are two which have traditionally been emphasized: they give advice to those who exercise control of the political arm of the executive branch on the content of policy; they may also be responsible for implementing it. The implementation of policy is carried out at all levels of government and includes the delivery of a service to the public (such as the payment of welfare benefits).

Civil service influence over policy making

In theory, senior civil servants give advice to politicians but the latter make decisions. The role of the civil service then becomes that of implementing these decisions. The key issue concerns the extent to which the provision of advice by senior civil servants enables them to dominate the policy-making process. It is argued that the role of civil servants sometimes goes beyond the mere provision of advice and entails the exertion of a considerable degree of influence over the content of public policy. Civil servants act both as policy makers and as policy implementers.

The accusation that civil servants usurped (took over without lawful authority) the role which ought to be fulfilled by politicians within the executive branch of government has been voiced in the UK in recent years. An extreme form of this argument has been that senior civil servants might conspire to prevent ministers from pursuing a course of action which they wished to embark upon.

Political control of the bureaucracy

There are various ways whereby the operations of the bureaucracy can be made susceptible to political control. Ministers may appoint their own advisers to offset the activities of civil servants. One problem is that if these advisers are outsiders they may effectively be 'frozen out' of the operations of a department by its permanent officials. In France, this difficulty is solved by ministers appointing existing civil servants to act as their advisers. These are located in the *cabinet ministériel*. They operate under the minister's direct control and usually revert to their previous posts when their service to the minister has ended.

Chief executives may also seek to exert influence over civil service actions. They may do this through involvement in the appointment, promotion and removal of civil servants. A major difficulty with these activities is that the civil service might become politicized. This means it becomes so closely identified with the policies of a particular political party that its neutrality (which is essential if it is to serve governments of other political persuasions) is questioned.

The legislature may also exert influence over the conduct of the bureaucracy. (This function is termed 'oversight' in America.) In the United Kingdom, special investigations may be launched by bodies such as parliamentary select committees into the operations of particular departments or agencies.

In assessing the effectiveness of political control over the bureaucracy, however, we must be aware of a potential conflict between accountability and managerial freedom. Although those whose activities are financed by public money need to account for what they do, excessive accountability tends to stifle initiative and make civil servants operate in a cautious manner dominated by adherence to stipulated procedures. Ideally, therefore, agencies should be accountable for their results but given a degree of discretion as to how these are achieved.

the
legislative
branch of
government

In this chapter we examine the work performed by the legislative branch of government. Although the main function of these bodies is to pass law, they carry out other responsibilities and in this chapter we consider the range of activities performed by legislatures and discuss the way in which they operate.

The way in which legislatures are organized differs from one country to another. One key distinction is that in some countries the legislature is composed of just one debating chamber whereas in others (such as the United Kingdom and the United States of America) it is comprised of two distinct bodies. The former is referred to as a 'unicameral' structure and the latter is termed 'bicameral'. In this chapter we consider the strengths and weaknesses of these different arrangements. We then discuss some of the problems that have affected both the power and authority of contemporary legislatures.

Elected legislatures are viewed as the symbol of representative government: as it is not possible for all citizens to directly share in policy making, they elect persons who perform these duties on their behalf. These representatives convene in the country's legislature (which is referred to as Congress in America, Parliament in the United Kingdom or the *Oireachtas* in Ireland). This is thus the institution that links the government and the governed. In addition to this symbolic function, legislatures undertake a number of specific tasks which we consider now.

Law making

Legislatures constitute the law-making body within a country's system of government. Thus making the law (or amending or repealing it) is a key function which they perform. A specific, although important, aspect of this role is approving the budget and granting authority for the collection of taxes.

A key issue concerns the extent to which legislatures themselves initiate law or respond to proposals put forward by the executive branch of government. There is a tendency for legislatures to respond to the initiatives of the executive branch in both presidential and parliamentary systems of government (thus transforming the legislature into a body which legitimizes decisions rather than one which initiates them).

Scrutiny of the executive

In addition to law making, legislatures scrutinize the actions of the executive branch of government. Governments are required to justify their actions to the legislature, which may thus exert influence over the government's conduct. This scrutiny may be retrospective (that is, it occurs after a decision has been implemented and seeks to examine whether it was justified). In some cases, however, the legislature may be required to give its consent to an action which the executive branch wishes to undertake. In America, for example, Congress has to approve a declaration of war.

In parliamentary systems in which the legislature provides the personnel of government, scrutiny facilitates ministerial responsibility. Governments are collectively responsible to the legislature. Perceived deficiencies in the overall activities of the government may result in its dismissal by the legislature (usually through the mechanism of a vote of 'no confidence'). Individual ministers may also be individually responsible for the performance of specific aspects of the work of the executive branch.

Confirmation of governmental appointments

Scrutiny may also extend to approving the nomination of individual members of the government put forward by the chief executive. This form of legislative scrutiny operates in some parliamentary systems of government such as Ireland. The scrutiny of nominations for public office by the legislature is also a feature of some presidential systems of government such as America, where the Senate is required to confirm a wide range of presidential appointments. The rationale for such a process is to ensure that those nominated for high government office have the relevant credentials to occupy such a post.

Investigatory functions

The investigation of issues of public importance is an important function of many legislative bodies, which is usually performed by committees. This role may be separate from the exercise of scrutiny over the actions of the executive. In America, Congress has the right to subpoena: that is, to force persons to appear and answer questions on the topic which is the subject of investigation and to secure the production of documents to aid the investigatory process.

Supervisory functions

Legislatures may concern themselves with the manner in which an institution of government or an activity that is reliant on public funds is being performed. This function (which in America is termed 'oversight') is concerned with monitoring the bureaucracy and its administration of policy. This entails ensuring that an agency is meeting the goals specified for it, that the public money provided for it is being spent for the purposes for which it was intended or that an operation is being conducted in accordance with any restrictions which were initially placed upon it by the legislature. The American Congress actively performs supervisory functions through committee hearings and the review of agency budgets, but these procedures are less prominent in other legislatures such as Britain.

Raising issues of local and national importance

Legislatures debate policy and other issues of public importance. Such debates are published in official journals and through the media, thus providing a source of information for the general public. This enables the electorate to be politically informed and educated. These bodies further provide a forum in which representatives can advance the interests of their constituencies and intercede on behalf of any of their constituents who have encountered problems in their dealings with the executive branch of government. Much work of this nature takes place in private, but it is usually possible to raise such issues publicly, within the legislative chamber.

Judicial functions

Legislatures may also perform judicial functions whereby members of all three branches of government may be tried and sentenced in connection with offences connected with the performance of their official duties. Legislatures may also exercise judicial-type functions in relation to the conduct of their members. The processes used vary.

Initiating constitutional change

Legislatures play a key role in the process of changing a country's constitution. In countries with a flexible constitution (that is, one which can be altered by the normal law-making process) the legislature is solely responsible for initiating and determining constitutional change. This is the situation in the United Kingdom. In countries with rigid constitutions (where amendment involves a separate process from the normal law-making procedure), the role of the legislature in providing for change is reduced.

The operations of legislatures

Legislatures conduct their affairs through a number of mechanisms.

Debate

Legislatures are first and foremost debating institutions. This means that functions such as the consideration of legislation, the articulation of constituency issues or the discussion of matters of national importance are performed orally. Members of the legislature deliver speeches in which they put forward their views and listen to the judgements of their fellow legislators on the same issue. To facilitate debate, members of legislative bodies may enjoy certain immunities which ordinary members of the general public do not possess. In the UK, for example, members of the House of Commons enjoy freedom of speech.

Committees

Much of the work performed by contemporary legislative bodies is delegated to committees. In turn, these bodies may devolve responsibilities to sub-committees, which have become increasingly influential in the US Congress since the 1970s. These are useful devices as they enable a legislature to consider a number of matters at the same time and thus cope with increased volumes of work associated with the expanded role of the state in years following the Second World War and membership of supranational bodies. They further enable small groups of legislators to investigate the affairs of government in considerable detail, and through their reports the entire assembly becomes more knowledgeable of these matters and thus less dependent on government for the provision of information.

Questions

Questions are a further means through which the work of the legislature is transacted in countries with parliamentary forms of government. These may be oral or written and are addressed to members of the executive branch of government. They can be of use in eliciting information, clarifying an issue or seeking to secure action by the executive branch of government, although they are rarely of importance to the process of policy making. They provide a mechanism whereby civil servants (who prepare the answers to these questions) respond to an agenda set by legislators as opposed to members of the executive branch of government.

Bicameral and unicameral legislatures

In most liberal democratic political systems, the legislature is divided into two separate bodies. These bodies form separate debating chambers. For example, in the United Kingdom parliament consists of the House of Commons and the House of Lords. In America, the legislative branch is divided into the House of Representatives and the Senate. In Ireland, parliament (the *Oireachtas*) consists of the *Dáil éireann* and the *Seanad éireann*, while in France the legislative function of government is shared between the National Assembly and the Senate. All these countries have what is termed a bicameral legislature.

The opposite of this is a unicameral system in which the legislature consists of only one body. Examples of this are found in New Zealand, Finland, Denmark, Sweden and Israel.

A revising chamber

An important benefit of a bicameral legislature is that one chamber can give the other an opportunity to think again, to reconsider its position. On occasions when the content of legislation is contentious and the period surrounding its passage through the first of the legislative bodies is charged with emotion for and against the measure, it is useful that a second chamber can coolly and calmly re-evaluate what has been done and if necessary invite the first chamber to reassess the situation by either rejecting the measure or proposing amendments to it. In this case, the second performs the function of a revising chamber.

Differences in composition

In bicameral systems, the two chambers of the legislature are often drawn from different constituencies (that is, composed in different ways). This may be an advantage in that it enables issues to be examined from different perspectives.

In some countries one chamber of the legislature is designed to represent public opinion while the other is concerned with territorial representation – advancing the more localized views of the areas, states or regions into which the country is divided. This was originally the justification for creating the American Senate.

The resolution of disagreements in bicameral legislatures

It is inevitable that disputes between the bodies that compose a bicameral legislature will sometimes arise. These situations are usually catered for in a country's constitution or by political practices that seek to avoid a situation in which one chamber effectively vetoes the work of the other, which results in total inaction. Let us consider some examples.

In the United Kingdom the two chambers of parliament are not co-equal in power and, in the case of disagreement between them, the views of the directly elected House of Commons will ultimately prevail. This situation is provided for in the 1949 Parliament Act, which gave the House of Lords the power to delay the progress of non-financial legislation which has been passed by the House of Commons for the maximum period of one year (spread across two parliamentary sessions), after which (provided the measure is reintroduced in the House of Commons) it will become law.

However, in America the two branches of the legislature are equal in status. The introduction of direct election for senators in 1913 resulted in both Houses of Congress being popularly elected.

Disagreements between the two chambers on legislation are resolved through the mechanism of a conference committee. If a bill is passed in different versions by the two Houses, a committee composed of members of each House is appointed to resolve the differences and draw up a single bill which is then returned to each House for a vote. Should either house reject this bill, it is returned to the conference committee for further deliberation.

Changes affecting the power and authority of legislatures

Developments have taken place in a number of countries that have had an adverse effect on the ability of legislatures to perform the functions outlined earlier in this chapter. These include:

Membership of supranational bodies

The membership of supranational bodies has resulted in the loss of some of parliament's traditional legislative functions.

Developments devaluing the law-making role of legislatures

The role of legislatures as law-making bodies has been undermined by a number of contemporary developments. These include aspects of 'people politics' in which citizens seek to secure changes in legislation by engaging in various forms of protest.

The role of the media

The ability of legislatures to scrutinize the actions of the executive, to air grievances or to educate the public concerning political affairs is often more effectively conducted by the media.

Domination by the executive branch of government

A major explanation for the decline in the power of legislatures is the tendency for these bodies to be dominated by the executive branch of government. In many countries, the initiation of policy and the control over finance has passed to the executive branch. It may subsequently be able to influence the detailed content of legislation, but is not the driving force behind it.

The economic climate

Public confidence in legislatures may be especially affected by the economic climate. Recession is further likely to reduce the capacity of institutions of government to act as innovators: rather than act as dynamic proponents of reform (which may enhance the standing of such bodies in the public eye) both executives and legislators are disposed towards inaction and to pruning public spending. This is a less adventurous exercise than initiating new programmes and may have an adverse effect on the way in which the public view the legislature.

Sleaze

Sleaze describes the abuse of power by elected public officials who improperly exploit their office for personal gain, party advantage (which may especially benefit party leaders to secure or retain their hold on power) or for sexual motives. The term also embraces attempts to cover up such inappropriate behaviour either by those guilty of misconduct or by their political colleagues.

One example of this occurred in the United Kingdom in 2009 when a national newspaper published details of MPs' expense accounts. Although in most cases MPs had broken no law relating to their expense claims, public opinion was concerned regarding the wide range of expenses which an MP could legitimately claim for.

the judiciary
and law
enforcement

The last branch of government we shall consider is the judiciary and in this chapter we will discuss the organization of the criminal courts in the United Kingdom and the manner in which criminal trials are conducted. We will then examine the operations of judicial systems and the roles that they perform in connection with the administration of various forms of law.

This chapter draws particular attention to the work of judges and the manner whereby their interpretation of the law may result in them assuming functions commonly associated with the legislative branch of government. Finally, the chapter draws particular attention to the political environment that may influence the way in which judges perform their duties.

No two liberal democratic countries have an identical judicial system. Differences especially exist concerning the conduct of trials. The UK and America utilize the adversarial system, in which two parties seek to prove their case by discrediting that put forward by their opponents. The trial is presided over by a judge whose main function is to ensure fair play. Many European countries utilize an inquisitorial system. Here the gathering of evidence is the responsibility of the judge and the main function of the trial is to resolve issues uncovered in the earlier investigation. The judge will actively intervene in the trial in order to arrive at the truth.

The organization of the courts in England and Wales

The civil and criminal courts in England and Wales are organized in a hierarchical fashion.

Most criminal cases are tried in magistrates' courts, the majority of which are staffed by laypersons termed 'justices of the peace'. The more serious cases, carrying heavier sentences, are heard in crown courts presided over by a judge and making use of a jury. Appeals against the verdicts reached in crown courts are heard by the Court of Appeal (Criminal Division).

Most civil cases which go to court are heard by county courts, although the High Court of Justice may hear cases in which large sums of money are claimed. Appeals against a verdict reached in a county court or the High Court will be heard by the Court of Appeal (Civil Division).

The House of Lords formerly acted as the final court of appeal for both criminal and civil cases. The 2005 Constitutional Reform Act replaced the jurisdiction of the House of Lords with a new body, the Supreme Court, which became operational in 2009. This court is composed of 12 justices and hears appeals on points of law for all civil cases in the UK and relating to criminal cases in England, Wales and Northern Ireland. It also adjudicates on devolution issues arising from the 1998 Scotland Act, the 1998 Northern Ireland Act and the 2006 Government of Wales Act.

Trial by jury

Juries are designed to provide a trial by one's peers (that is, equals) and they are an important feature of the judicial process in the UK and America. In the UK, jurors are chosen from the electoral register drawn up by local government. Their role is to listen to the evidence that is put forward in a trial by the defence and prosecution and come to a decision as to whether the defendant is guilty or not guilty.

Juries possess a number of advantages. Their ability to pronounce a 'not guilty' verdict in the face of overwhelming evidence to the contrary may bring about reform of the law if public opinion feels that the law and the penalties that it imposes are unjust. Juries may also take the motive of the lawbreaker into account when deciding on his or her guilt or innocence.

Nonetheless, there are problems associated with juries. They are not necessarily socially representative and this may lead to perceptions that racial or gender bias underpins their decisions. It is also possible that jurors may be swayed by the conduct of lawyers, which poses the problem that rich people can hire the most effective performers in court, effectively buying their acquittal from crimes they have committed.

Administrative law

Administrative law is concerned with the relationship between a government and its citizens. In the United Kingdom challenges mounted by the general public to the actions or operations of the executive branch of government may be heard in the courts. The legality of delegated legislation or accusations of abuse of power may be challenged in this manner. Minor issues (such as a challenge to a decision taken by a civil servant) may, however, be resolved by tribunals. Complaints of maladministration (that is, an accusation that incorrect procedures were followed to arrive at a decision) may be submitted to the ombudsman.

In other countries, however, a separate court system exists to adjudicate upon such matters. Germany and France have a distinct system of courts concerned with administrative law.

Constitutional law

In some countries the courts may be also called upon to adjudicate disputes arising from the constitution. This is termed 'judicial review'. Typically, it involves assessing whether Acts passed by the legislature accord with the statement of fundamental law contained in a country's constitution. But it may also scrutinize actions undertaken by the executive branch (such as the executive orders issued by the American president). If the courts decide that such actions are in breach of the constitution, they may be declared 'unconstitutional'. This has the effect of overturning them: they are rendered 'null and void'.

In America, the process of judicial review is performed by the Supreme Court. This consists of nine judges appointed by the president subject to the consent of the Senate. Their intervention occurs when cases are referred to them on appeal either from the highest courts of appeal in the states or from the federal court of appeal. Judicial review provides the Supreme Court with considerable political power.

A country that lacks a codified constitution (such as the UK) does not have any process whereby the actions of bodies such as parliament can be overturned. This procedure would be contrary to the concept of the sovereignty of parliament. This doctrine insists that parliament is the sole source of law-making power whose actions cannot be overruled by any other body. In countries with uncodified constitutions, judicial review has a more limited scope, that of scrutinizing the actions undertaken by the legislature, executive or other tiers of government to ensure that they accord with the requirements imposed upon them by legislation.

Judicial interpretation

In theory, the role of judges is to apply the law or the constitution to the matter that comes before them. However, it is often argued that judges go beyond this role and effectively determine its contents, which are subsequently binding on courts dealing with similar cases. This situation arises as a result of judicial interpretation of such documents, which may effectively give judges the ability to act in a law-making capacity.

Judicial interpretation may help to ensure that the law or constitution is kept up to date or accords with changing public sentiments as to what constitutes reasonable conduct. However, critics of this role argue that judges ought to distinguish between interpreting the law and actually writing it. They assert that judicial interpretation leads judges to perform a role which ought to be carried out by the legislative branch of government or through the process of constitutional amendment.

The politics of the judiciary

We know from our own experiences that it is difficult to act in a totally detached and neutral manner. Our actions are likely to be based upon our personal values. Judges are no exception to this. The following section evaluates some of the factors that might influence the way in which judges discharge their responsibilities and the extent to which they are sufficiently accountable for their actions.

Personal values

The personal values of judges may exert considerable influence on the way in which they perform their duties. These values may be influenced by factors including the judges' social background or legal training. If judges are socially unrepresentative they may be open to the accusation of discriminatory conduct towards those from a different background.

Political opinions

The political opinions held by a judge may also influence how that official operates. These may derive from the position which the judiciary occupies in the machinery of the state. In a liberal democracy judges may regard the preservation of this system of government to be of paramount importance. This may influence the attitude which judges display in cases when state interests are involved. Alternatively, these opinions may consist of the judge's own political preferences. In many countries the executive branch of government has the ability to appoint judges. In America, for example, presidents often seek to promote their political values through the appointments they make to the federal judicial system especially to the Supreme Court. They appoint judges to these positions whose political views mirror their own.

Judicial accountability

We have suggested that the personal views of judges and political considerations might influence the way in which the courts operate. If we accept that judges are able to inject personal or political biases into their work, especially when interpreting the law or constitution, we need to examine the sufficiency of mechanisms through which judges can be made to explain and justify their actions and, if necessary, be punished for them.

In a liberal democracy members of the legislative and executive branches of government (who in theory are charged with initiating and carrying out legislation) are accountable for their actions. Judges, however, are usually insulated from any direct form of political accountability for their actions, even when these have a fundamental bearing on political affairs. They are usually unelected (although this method of appointment does apply in some American states) and once appointed enjoy security of tenure.

There are, however, some formal controls over the activities of judges. These include the ability of politicians to intervene in the operations of the criminal justice system (which in the UK includes legislation setting out a wide range of mandatory sentences which judges are required to implement). The use of juries may help to offset judicial biases. The decisions of judges can also be set aside by a successful appeal to a higher court, revision to the law or an amendment to the constitution.

www.ingramcontent.com/pod-product-compliance
Ingram Content Group UK Ltd.
Pitfield, Milton Keynes, MK11 3LW, UK
UKHW021828270225
455667UK00014B/157